PERSIANS

Aeschylus

PERSIANS

in a new version by

Kaite O'Reilly

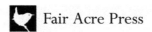 Fair Acre Press

Fair Acre Press

First published in Great Britain in 2019 by Fair Acre Press
www.fairacrepress.co.uk

A catalogue record for this book is available from the British Library

ISBN 978-1-911048-38-1

Cover photo: Gerald Tyler, John Rowley and Richard Huw Morgan in National Theatre Wales production of Kaite O'Reilly's *Persians*, directed by Mike Pearson. © Toby Farrow

Cover Design and Typeset by Nadia Kingsley

About Kaite O'Reilly

Kaite O'Reilly is a multi award-winning writer and dramaturg whose body of work includes poetry, prose, radio drama, screen and theatre.

www.kaiteoreilly.com

Other books by Kaite O'Reilly

Atypical Plays for Atypical Actors (Oberon)

The 'd' Monologues (Oberon)

Woman of Flowers (Aurora Metro)

Henhouse (Oberon)

peeling (faber & faber)

peeling in *Graeae Plays 1: Redefining Disability*
(Aurora Metro)

Editor of *FACE ON: Disability Arts in Ireland and Beyond*
(ADI/Create)

Winner of the Ted Hughes Award for New Work in Poetry

Judges Gillian Clarke, Stephen Raw and Jeanette Winterson awarded the Ted Hughes Award for New Work in Poetry to Kaite O'Reilly for her extraordinary retelling of Aeschylus' play, The Persians.

"Poetry crosses time, the old play becomes the new poetry. Here's the truth of language colliding with the clichés of politics and the advertisement of war."

Judges of the Ted Hughes Award

"Persians is a beautifully poetic version of Aeschylus' tragic play. Kaite O'Reilly's masterly retelling of this 2,500 year old story focuses on how war destroys people's identity and her use of language is contemporary but never loses any of the historical context."

The Poetry Society

Introduction

Persians by Aeschylus is the oldest extant verse drama in the Western canon. First presented at Athens' City Dionysia Festival in 472 BCE, it recounts the Persian response to military defeat at the Battle of Salamis in 480 BCE.

Aeschylus: poet, philosopher, soldier-playwright, anti-warmonger, humanist. He chose to write about an astonishing, almost miraculous event, a David and Goliath of its day: the spectacular and relatively recent defeat of the marauding Persian Imperial force by the people of Athens. Aeschylus was an Athenian. He could have written a swaggering tale of victory, of the battle-prowess Greeks and their cunning and sacrifice to protect this early, emerging experiment in (a form of) democracy. He could have written a xenophobic pageant of blood-lust and warriors, filled with self-congratulatory jingoism and gloating over the dead. Instead – in my reading at least – he chose to write a powerful anti-war verse drama which painfully depicts the waste and agonies of conflict – what Wilfred Owen, another soldier-poet, called 'the pity of war' – written with fire and dignity from the point of view of the defeated.

This perspective drew me to the text. For some years in the mid-1990's fellow dramatist Christina Katic and I volunteered for Suncokret, a nonpartisan grassroots humanitarian relief aid organisation led by people displaced by war in former Yugoslavia. We worked in frontline towns during the war and through the post war reconstruction. I started the first of my anti-war plays, *YARD*, when under missile attack in a makeshift shelter in an orphanage in the Krajina in 1995. In a lull in the shelling the next morning, Chris and I were evacuated out of Karlovac during what became known as Operation Storm, the largest European land battle since the Second World War. Although my experience of conflict was slight, it impacted profoundly on my world-view, politics, and the material I wanted to write. In 2002 I premiered my second anti-war piece, *peeling*. Years later John E McGrath, then artistic director of National Theatre Wales, approached me about writing a new verse version of *Persians* for the company's inaugural year. Apart from long being an admirer of Aeschylus and, indeed, the production's director, Mike Pearson, I was keen for *Persians* to be the final part of my anti-war trilogy.

*

"There is no exact correlation between languages. This process becomes even more difficult and contingent when you're translating between times as well, there is no exact correlation between periods." Colin Teevan.

'My' *Persians* is not a translation. I don't know Ancient Greek, so am unable to read the text in the original. My starting point was several literal translations which I pored over, line by line, assisted by a Greek linguist friend over many cups of coffee. I briefly engaged with some Classicists who were all in robust dialogue with one another, but determined I followed 'their' individual perspective. This encouraged me to widen my research and to read as much as possible, although each version was filled with the predilections, biases and values of the times the poet/translator lived in. I hoped to ascertain through this strange act of ventriloquism the echo of what might have been Aeschylus. Despite the palimpsest nature of reworking ancient texts, if twenty translations used a particular image or metaphor, I hoped this might be a trace of the original imagination.

I read many 're-imaginings', scripts where the expansionist Persian force was reinterpreted respectively as Hitler, Saddam Hussein, and Bush Senior and Junior. There was blood over land, blood over oil and a post-apocalyptic Twenty-second century version with blood over water. There was unintelligible slang, rhyming couplets, heroic hexameter, and complex poetic schemas which failed to keep my interest. I tried to read the farce with songs, but there's a limit even to my love of research.

I soon settled into reading direct translations, asking myself what was happening socially or culturally in each case to warrant – or demand – a 'new' version.

I read Victorian versions stiff with flounces and patriotic, indigestible poetry foreshadowing the death of Empire; post-dramatic versions where the language was so spare it was all but flayed from the body of the original narrative; and brave Modernist inter-war versions, decrying war whilst anticipating another. I began to pay attention to the year the translation was made in order to comprehend the socio-political times in which it was written.

What became apparent very quickly was the sense of a long line of practitioners who had, over the ages, thrown their hat into the ring and made 'their' version of this great classic, informed, if not provoked, by the age through which they lived. There was always something that warranted a new translation or production of this particular text – invariably the anticipation of, the participation in, the protesting against, or the recovery from a long, bloody, and in many cases, unnecessary conflict. During my reading I had a constant sense of déjà vu, with each writer responding to their own times with the ageless story of *Persians*. It was also humbling to sense this rope of 'new' versions reaching back to the first millennia BCE, and strangely emotional to think that in my own small way, I would be joining it.

My own experience was writing a verse version for Mike Pearson's site-specific production on Ministry of Defence

land in the Welsh Brecon Beacons. At that time soldiers
were being trained there before being deployed to
Afghanistan and Iraq – geographically part of the former
Persian empire. The text was performed in Sennybridge
Training area, with the audience coached-in from
barracks by army personnel. They gathered at a 'rally'
before promenading through purpose-built village
FIBUA – Fighting In Built Up Areas – created, to use the
military parlance, 'in order to rehearse the theatre of
war'. The final location was a firing range, a large
building missing the fourth wall, like an opened doll's
house, opposite which the audience sat, watching the
action within. I remember the young squaddies, having
completed their day of training in this wild and remote
landscape, gathering in the shadows to observe our
production, and the distant explosions and gunfire that
punctuated the dress rehearsal. One of the soldiers told
me he was being deployed to 'Afghan' later that week,
and this training was to prepare him for facing conflict.
Thereafter the performances were haunted (both in my
mind and actuality) by those 'going out to serve' on the
landmass that was formerly part of the Persian empire.

*

The text that follows is newly revised and re-structured
for publication, designed for ease of reading as poetry
rather than experienced as promenade live performance.
I chose to break the chorus into three identifiable figures:
head of state, head of the church (such as an archbishop)

and head of the military. I have included some numbered line references which relate to the Ancient Greek but owing to the dramaturgical amendments for ease of reading these are not always numerically consistent. I retain them for reference. I have echoed the form of the original insofar as I can ascertain it through my reading of twenty-three texts composed over three centuries – a mix of prose and poetic schema devised, I like to think, by Aeschylus himself. I have included various versions of asides, calls and laments as side-text, and settled on one spelling of place names and persons although there are often multiple variations available. These, along with historical references and identification of personae I leave to the scholars and other publications. I enter this endeavour as a poet and a dramatist, in dialogue with that first great poet-soldier. Any errors are of course entirely my own.

Kaite O'Reilly. 2019

PERSIANS

Chorus 1
The bloom of the Persian land is gone.

Chorus 2
We have emptied ourselves of young men,

hurled the blossom of youth after one last sortie.

Now, peopled solely by women, the old, and infirm

we wait, stoic but silent, as the days

lengthen into another endless night

with no news.

Chorus 1
None?

Chorus 2
I'm afraid.

My heart spasms like some nightmare thing

stuck its claws into my chest and squeezed.

Chorus 1
No news yet of the campaign?
Chorus 3
No.

Chorus 1
Are the lines down?
Chorus 3
No.

Chorus 1
Then why no word?

Chorus 3

We know there is demand for news of the campaign.

Chorus 2   10

Rumour is rife. Hearts scalded with apprehension.

Chorus 3

Patience.

Intelligence is thin but will be forthcoming.

Chorus 2   100

Is it a trick? Have we walked into a trap,

some celestial snare men cannot break?

What mortal can escape divine cunning?

Whose step so light he can leap across it?

Have we been lulled, coaxed by apparent goodwill

into the net of ruin, which no one survives unscathed?

I'm sorry.

Forgive me,

these are the fears that shroud my mind,   115

darken my heart with dread.

I'm pierced through,

lacerated with terror for the Persian armament;

stabbed with dread for our absent sons

whose very absence leaves us vulnerable.

Chorus 3

Never let these ancient city stones

ring out in lament for us and our young men.

Nor the Kissian walls resound with women keening,

fists beating heads and breasts.

Chorus 2

Never let Susa's wide streets in the late afternoon

be alive with death

and the meticulous rending of cloth,

fingers busy shredding fine linen:

our women, Persia's women,   *125*

naked with grief.

Chorus 3

For our youth have left the hive

to the humming swarm of battle

across the narrow bridge of boats

that binds each neck of land together: *130*

marching, riding, driving, gone.

Chorus 2

And the Persian women watch after them,

gazing on the distance

where the dust has long settled,

longing for their men

in the suddenly too-big beds,

regretting the speed with which they hurled

their furious spear-armed mates into conflict.

Chorus 3

That was their sacrifice, their selfless battle cry.

Chorus 2

Which is now merely tears

as they weep out

the abject loneliness of their days.

Chorus 1

Victory is inevitable.

Failure is not in our language.

The term was expunged from common use

the moment our boys set out for Athens.

Chorus 3

We are invincible

and any doubt is traitor to our cause.

Just think of the numbers,

the power, the prowess

pouring forth from Susa,

Agbatana, Kissia!

We stood here and watched it pass –

the juice of Asia,

our adrenaline-fuelled youth

spiked for adventure,

eager to see the world

and obtain it.

Those slick cogs primed

in one killing machine

– ours –   20

obedient to Amistres, Artaphernes,

Marshalls of the Persians,

Megabazes, Astapes:

great generals all,

loyal to one king of kings.   25

How can we fail?

Thousands upon thousands

of soldiers, cavalry, seamen –

armed, trained, resolved

and ready for action.

The world gazes upon our might

and trembles.

Chorus 1

What we know is a two-pronged attack,

by land and sea set forth, led by Artembares

and his armoured car, vehicle of death.   *30*

Chorus 3

Then came Masistres, flanked

by the skilled marksman Imaeus,

Sosthanes with his formidable horse power,

and Pharandaces, who shows no fear.

Chorus 1

We stood here and watched them pass:

the Nile marching as one,

deployed from every corner of the Empire.

Highly skilled oarsmen from the Egyptian marshes

thronged in unimaginable numbers

too vast to behold.   *40*

Chorus 3

Sardis, famous for its precious metal reserves

sent horse-drawn chariots armoured with gold

in squadrons three, four and six abreast.

A brilliant sight, it dazzled us,

war machinery crowding for battle.

Chorus 1
Eager to sling the yoke of slavery upon the Greeks

were Mysian javeliners, anvil-hard,

their strength as manifest as spears.

Chorus 3
Then in a column from glittering Babylon

marines and marksmen

sure in their prowess, confidence

bristling with numbers.

Chorus 1
Blades drawn and glinting,

the force of Asia's military might

answering their young master's call.   *59*

Chorus 3
What we know from intelligence is

the crossing was made over the strait to Europe   *66*

in an audacious display of skill and daring.

Bark bound to bark,

the infamous Hellespont yoked

with a floating bridge   70

– a road of boats –

bow lashed to bow, timbers laid across.

A highway to battle

over which Xerxes, Asia's commander,

drove his warring thousands

in twofold armament:

by land, by sea, on foot, by horse.

Undefeatable.

Chorus 2

Word from the ground hailed this miracle of Xerxes

the equal of the gods!

Chorus 1

Eyes glistening dark with intent for murder:

Xerxes, warlord,

fierce as a dragon scaled in gold.

Chorus 3

There is no resisting this force,

as futile as fighting a hurricane, the sea.   90

Who dares stand against the iron storm of our arrows,

the tempest of our military might – and remains standing?

Chorus 1

Their useless lances against our airborne spears.

Death rains down on them.

Chorus 3

No one can withstand this rampaging flood,

the tsunami of the Persians in full rage.

We are irresistible.

Chorus 1

For we are the lucky ones.

It has been our fortune and our fate to be so blessed,

our birthright to plunder, to lay low the strong towers,

storm cities, expand our horizons.   104

We are a warrior people who,

since ancient times, have ravished the earth.

Chorus 2

And our gods have looked down on us
and smiled.

Chorus 3

We have learned faith in the blade.
To stare, as now, fathoms deep
to where the sea whitens   110
beneath the tempest's blast.
And to trust in our ships –
the fine cables, cords of flax, to hold firm   113
and bear the burden of our sons, across.

Chorus 1

For what you see before you is
embodied trust.
Survival has its benefits:
position, command, authority,
and we acquit ourselves well,
we understudies to power,
rulers by proxy for the warring Xerxes,
son of Darius, inheritor of Empire.
For what is our land but a cloth of gold
spun and respun from the yarns

of overland sorties?

And we watch the spinning.

We've done well,

rewarded in our wisdom and our age

with trust.   7

The trust to govern in the absence of our king.

Chorus 2   148

But look, the Queen approaches, radiant.

Let us greet and revere her, as is fit.

~Queen enters~

Chorus 1

Most reverent of women, our first Lady of noble birth,

consort to Darius, the God of Persians,

and mother to a god, too,

unless the Fates have turned their faces from us

and our army's ancient fortune now fails.

Queen

That, too, is my fear.

I'm driven from the palace, its golden rooms 160

and bedchamber I shared with Darius shine

like blinded mirrors, reflecting nothing,

for the eye of the house, the master, is not here.

I feel the canker-fret of care.*

This plucking at my heart – a twofold care –

as newfound doubts divide my mind.

It is an anxiety I can barely utter, but which must 165

be voiced, counsellors, even if to purge.

We should not confuse true prosperity

with material possessions.

I fear that this grasp for wealth may trample

and kick to dust the peace and true prosperity

Darius secured with divine help.

For money without men is insecure

and men without money are undervalued

and an uneasy peace sits between these truths.

Is the royal purse secure without

the presence of the eye – the master –

the one who acquired and preserved its munificence? *170*

Kind and faithful elders, give me your advice

on what I am about to say,

for on your good counsel, all security rests.

Chorus 2

Majesty, in words and in deeds

we are at your service –

willingly, and dutifully,

our allegiance and power are yours.

Queen   *176*

Since my son raised his army and set out to lay Greece

to waste, I have been visited by persistent dreams, but

none as vivid and troubling as the one I had last night.

Two women appeared to me: one in Persian robes,   *180*

the other in Dorian dress – both striking in stature

and beauty, flawless in their loveliness.

They were clearly sisters of the same descent but each

with her own inheritance: one allotted and living

in Greece, the other in the East.

And between them there seemed to rise

a disagreement, a quarrel that escalated into a rage
which my son witnessed and tried to calm.   *190*
He decided to restrain the women and make them live
side by side as friends.

So he harnessed them to his chariot,
lashing their necks to the yoke.

And the one dressed in Persian clothes stood tall
and proud, her mouth meek, tongue obedient
to the rein, but the other struggled and fought,
tearing up the tackle with both hands and, free
from the bit and bridle, she broke loose, snapping
the chariot pole, smashing the yoke and so my son
was thrown.

And he fell to the ground; he sprawled in the dust
as his father Darius stood watching on – pityingly.
And when Xerxes saw his father's piteous gaze,
he tore at his clothes, destroying them.

Such was my dream of last night.   *200*

When I woke, I washed my hands in flowing water

then, purified, went to pray for the deliverance from evil,

making rituals befitting to those powers that be.

And as I stood there, offering in hand,

I saw an eagle fly up to Apollo's altar.

Speechless I watched –

and then saw a falcon circling the air, a hawk,

which in a sudden rush of beating wings attacked

the eagle, tearing at its crown with vicious talons.

But the eagle did nothing to protect itself –

it submitted to the onslaught and bloodied wounds,

cowering as its head was ripped asunder.

Terrible to see, terrible to tell.

But have no doubt: if my son succeeds, and returns

victorious, he will be hailed a wonder –

if he fails, he is not answerable to the state.

He owes no explanations to the city or the people.

If he returns safely, he will rule the land, as before.

Chorus 1   *215*

Queen Mother, we neither wish to alarm you,
nor raise false hopes with what we say.

Chorus 2

When you next pray, ask the gods to avert
any misfortune you may have foreseen,
bringing instead every good for you,
your children and allies, and for Persia, too.
Then pour libations to the earth and the dead,
asking with an open, gracious heart
your late husband Darius, who you saw
in your dream last night, to send up blessings
to you and Xerxes from beneath the earth
and to contain in subterranean darkness
their opposite ills. This counsel comes
from a kind and sober heart, but, ill omens
or not, we predict things will turn out well,
and for the best.

Queen

Your reading of my dream shows

good intent and loyalty

both to my son Xerxes and the royal house.

May it be as you say!

I shall follow your good advice when I withdraw,

offering prayers to the powers above and to those

who love us, below.

But first, one question: This Athens... Where does it lie?

Chorus 3

A great distance from here.

Chorus 1

Far away, westwards, where the sun

declines and sets.

Queen

One town, so far away?

Why would my son so eagerly seek it out?

Chorus 3

If Lord Xerxes succeeds and Athens falls,

the entire landmass of Greece

will come under his control.

Queen

How great is their force, the numbers?

Chorus 1

Large enough to create problems in the past.

Chorus 3

We know them of old. We have clashed, before.

Queen   *237*

So what resources do they have? Sufficient wealth?

Chorus 2

A seam of silver running as a vein through the earth

is their national treasure.

Queen

And how do they fight? Are they great archers?

Is that the source of their strength and prowess?

Chorus 3

It's not the arrow's point or bow's sinewy strength

that makes them to be feared. They are close fighters,

hand to hand, heavily armoured, with targe and spear.

Queen

So who shepherds this force? Who is their warlord?

Chorus 1

No one.

Queen

No one?

Chorus 1

They bow the knee to none.

Queen

So how can they Marshall themselves, and stand against

an enemy attack?

Chorus 3

Well enough to crush Darius's great force, in the past.

Queen

Cruel words for those whose sons serve overseas.

Chorus 2

We will know all soon enough. Look: a man, running.

Chorus 3

A Persian soldier, by his bearing.

He will give us all – good or bad – straight.

~Messenger enters~

Messenger

Cities of Asia!

Loved Persian land,

once haven of great wealth: *250*

A single stroke has blasted all

our hopes and achievements.

Luck, prosperity, fortune – all gone.

The flower of Persian youth has perished;

crushed, snapped, severed from the root.

It's my curse being the bearer of such news,

but I must tell you:
Everything is lost.   *255*

Chorus 1
Everything?

Messenger
Everything.

Chorus 3
It's impossible.

Chorus 2
A stabbing under my ribs

Chorus 1
There's a mistake.

Messenger
There's no mistake.

Chorus 3
Fleet, army, troops?

Messenger
All lost.

Chorus 2

This pain. Across my chest

Chorus 1

All?

Everything from the expedition – utterly destroyed.

Chorus 3

No.

Messenger

I didn't expect to return alive.

Chorus 1

Some misinformation...?

Messenger

This is not hearsay. I was there.

I've lived too long to hear such news.

Messenger

I was there, an eye witness.

I can catalogue the horrors of defeat.

Chorus 3

The waste!

To travel so far, in vain...

To march only to death.

Messenger

The shores of Salamis and the dunes, behind,

are clogged with Persian dead.

Chorus 2   *274*

Our loved ones, drowned,

battledress their shroud.

Our children now bloated, bobbing,

mere flotsam in the careless sea.

Messenger

Our weapons were useless against the ceaseless

ramming of the ships.

Prow butted prow. We were helpless.

I watched an entire generation die.

Chorus 2

Cry out! Lament!

Persians, mourn.

The gods forsake us.

Our army, our future, ruined.

Messenger

Salamis, the most hated name.

Say Athens and weep.   284

Chorus 3

Athens: hateful to her enemies.

We remember the past, and Marathon:

Persian women stripped of their men.

Widowed. Childless. For nothing. Again.

Queen

I have listened senseless, witless,

struck silent with horror at this catastrophe.

The news is too terrible for questions

but question we must.   290

We are mortal and have no choice

but to bear the ills the gods bestow.

So speak.

Tell us all, calmly and plainly, despite your own grief.
Unfold our pain, unfurl this disaster in its entirety –
we will bear it.

Who is missing? Who died in action?
Who was appointed to command
but deserted, leaving his post unmanned?
Who, amongst our generals and our princes
must we mourn?
All?
Are there any not dead?

Messenger
Xerxes lives to see the light of day.

Queen   *300*
Your words are a bright comfort to me and the royal
house, breaking like dawn across the darkest of nights.

Messenger
But Artembares, leader of ten thousand cavalry
rolls in the tide, beaten against Sileniae's hard coast.

And Dedaces, the Chiliarch, lord of a thousand, fell   *305*

like a bird, speared mid-leap from his ship to the shore.

And Lord Tenagon of the Bactrians now tilts and drifts

along the shore of Ajax island. Lilaeus, Arsames

and Argestes, who were struggling in the fight

no longer struggle, flaying their sides against

the granite cliffs where the rock-doves nest.

And so too Pharnuchus and our allies from Egypt:

Arcteus, Adeues, Pheresseues who all fell speared

from one ship. Dead. And Matallus of Chrysa,

who led ten thousand of the Black cavalry,   *314*

his full shaggy beard dyed red in death, skin

brilliant crimson in a pool of blood.

And Arabos the Magus, dead.

Artabes the Bactrian, dead.

Leaders of thirty thousand horses,

immigrants to a harsh land, all dead.

And Amistres, and Amphistreus whose lethal spear

took many lives, gave up his own. And the arrows

of Ariomardus will make no more widows,   *320*

nor will Seisames the Mysian bring further grief.

Admiral Tharybis from Lyrna, who captained

five times fifty ships met a wretched end,   *325*

his once handsome face destroyed, now ugly in death.

And Syennesis, commanding the Cilician fleet,

who singlehandedly dealt most harm to the enemy,

outstanding in courage, died heroically.

Name after name.

These are just a few from the roll call of thousands.

Thousands upon thousands,

unimaginable suffering.

There are so many more. 330

Chorus 3

Too many.

Messenger

All dead.

Queen

Ai-ee!

This is the very peak of misery.

We think we reach the summit,

but it towers still above us.

I can already hear the shrill screaming of lament.

Of loss! Of shame.

We are disgraced. How is this possible?
Go back and begin again. Tell me. Exactly.

What were the numbers, the actual
numbers of the Greek fleet?

How strong was their force that they dared attack
the great Persian armada, relying solely
on the ram-thrusts of their ships?

Messenger

If numbers were all, the day would have been ours'.
The Greeks' entire fleet was three hundred ten,
with ten select warships a special reserve squadron.
Whereas Xerxes commanded one thousand sails
– Persian ships crowding the horizon –
I know this for a fact, with galleons, surpassing in speed
– the fastest vessels ever made –
two hundred seven more we held in account.
That is the exact reckoning.
We held the advantage, in all ways superior.
If numbers were all, we would not have failed.

Queen

Then how – ?

Messenger

A spirit, some divine power

must have adjusted the scales,

throwing the balance out, weighting

fortune against us.

How else could we fail?

The gods saved Athene's city.

Queen

Saved? It still stands? Athens remained unscathed?

Messenger

While the people live, the city defences are secure.

Queen   350

So tell us of the battle, how it began, this naval disaster.

Who struck first? The Greeks?

Or was it my son, revelling

in misplaced confidence in the glory of his fleet?

Messenger

It was a curse, your Majesty, some demon
or avenging power that ignited the fuse of our misery.

Queen

Tell me.

Messenger

A man appeared,
a Greek from the Athenian camp
who spoke to your son Xerxes.

He said the Greeks were nervous, understandably so
in the face of Persian might.
Their courage was deserting them and once night fell
they would, too, leaping on board to their posts
and rowing for their lives in disarray, in every direction,
their cowardice hidden under cover of darkness.   360

And Xerxes, unschooled in treachery and naive
to the jealousy of the gods, believed him.

He summoned the admiralty and charged them
with the following order: 365

As soon as the sun's rays stops

scorching the earth,

and darkness coats

the vaulted arc of the sky: Action stations!

They were to position the main body of the fleet

in three divisions:

One column to guard the exit routes from the bay

of Eleusis north of Salamis, a second

to patrol the straits to the eastern end; the other vessels

to encircle the island of Ajax, watching the western exit

from the bay, on the Megarian side.* The strategy

was to block all access to open water,

and should any Greek escape and slip through this net

by secret means: *370*

Your heads will pay for it.

Such was his decree to the Persian captains,

proudly, even lightly said.

For how could Xerxes know

what the gods had planned for him?

Our men were well trained and obedient.

They prepared their supper
and each sailor fixed his oar
neatly to the rowing pin.
Shipshape. Disciplined. Ordered. 375

When finally the sun sank and darkest night set in,
every master oarsman and armed marine
went onboard and sailed, as instructed, 380
calling out encouragement to one another,
line to line,
rank to rank,
keeping up morale,
keeping their position,
as assigned.

And we sailed back and forth, as commanded,
the whole night through, to and fro, across and back,
without resting, without ceasing, without one sign
of the Greeks.

And night seeped into dawn,
and with straining, tired eyes we saw on the horizon

pale horses galloping closer, whiter,

becoming brilliant bright light

and the day broke over us and still no sign –

but a sound.

A shout.

Echoing. Jangling. Terrible.

The clear, ringing song of triumph

from the Greeks. It shot across the bay,   *390*

reverberated, leaping back from the craggy cliffs.

And then we knew.

We knew.

Fear stood behind each man

and we cowered in its presence,

hope destroyed. Our plan had made us fools.

For this was not the shriek of flight,

but the rallying cry,

the rising sacred paen-song of battle.

And then their trumpet blazed

in our ears, calling them to arms,

and their oars beat the waves with a single pulse,
and the frenzied sea roared from this one command
and suddenly they were in sight, the right wing first,
leading the way, then the whole fleet following   *400*
to the attack, as arranged. And constantly, from every
throat, the command:

> *Liberation! Sons of Greece, to battle!*
> *For the freedom of your homeland, your children*
> *and wives, fight! For your ancestral gods,*
> *your forefathers' graves, all or nothing!*
> *Now is the time! Strike! All is at stake!*

From our side came an answering call.   *405*
And then they were upon us.

Ship smashed into ship with bronze prows, wood
splintering, the dull groan of impact. First blood
was to the Greeks, Ameinas of Pallene,[*]
whose warship snapped off the full curving stern
of a Phoenician vessel.   *410*
Men struck with their spears from both sides.
Now charge followed charge, each captain targeting

an enemy ship on which to ram his own.

At first the Persian fleet held firm, but we were choked

in the straits, hundreds of our ships crammed

in that narrow stretch of water, we were unable to move,

to help, to stop butting the sides of our own ships,

shattering our own oars, battering our own vessels

with the weaponry of our metal rams. And in the

horror of this helpless self-destruction,   *415*

the Greeks calmly circled,

orderly and efficient,

and then came in for the kill.

I saw wave upon wave of meat, bone, bodies.

A sea of flesh, of men, and the groaning sinking carcass

of our fleet. Ships overturned, hulls smashed,   *420*

and everywhere our men, face down, floating.

They littered the beaches, snagged on the rocks

and however many died, there was still more

for the Greeks to fillet, to thrash at in the water

with broken oars, like fish in a net. A whole shoal,

already rotting, in the roiling mass of the bloodied sea.

It was the noise that was the worst.

Even when night fell and hid the view

I could still hear the sounds of slaughter.

Thousands upon thousands. Their screams in the dark.

Thousands upon thousands. The moaning.

I could take days to tell, ten days, and still not tell all. *430*

Never

have so many died on one day.

Queen

Aiee!

An ocean of disaster has broken over the Persians,

washing away the whole eastern race.

Messenger

But I have only told part.

More is to come.

Double.

Worse.

Queen

Worse?

What more can you tell

to tilt this scale of misery?   *440*

Messenger

Those Persians in their prime,

the finest in courage and nobility,

our best, most choice, in loyalty

the king's own equals.

They have perished – killed with dishonour.

Queen

This is more than can be borne by one heart.

I am cursed, my friends.

Now tell me how they died.

Messenger

There is an island off the coast of Salamis,

small, with poor anchorage, a haunt of Pan,

whose hoof prints are reputed to pock the sand.

Xerxes sent the Persian princes there,

for safety, he thought,   450

to help our men, or finish off the enemy

taking refuge there from their sinking ships.

Easy prey, he thought.

Greeks would die.
Persians would live.
So he thought.

But when the gods gave victory to the Greeks,
that same day they surrounded the island,
clad themselves in fine bronze armour and leapt
from their ships, noosing the island in a circle of bronze
which grew smaller and tighter as they advanced.
The Persians had nowhere to turn.

First came a hail of stones, and then arrows,   *460*
and as the noose grew tighter, with one final surge,
the Greeks charged with swords, hacking, dismantling,
metal on bone, hewing limbs, butchering them all
until every last one was dead.

And on a high cliff, on the mainland,
and in clear sight of the killing fields
Xerxes saw all and howled.

And in plain view of the whole army
he ripped his clothes and wept, ordering:

Break ranks! Retreat! Run!

And then he turned, deserting, and fled,   470

heaping disaster on disaster.

And so we too ran.

Now, majesty,

you may weep.

Queen

God is cruel.

You hateful divinity,

how you beguiled our minds

and stole our wits

to exact this last punishment.

What the Greeks owed, my Xerxes paid.

Wasn't the dead at Marathon enough for you?   475

My son,

expecting the sweetness of revenge

is tainted now with bitterness.

He went to Athens to account and instead

has drawn down this sorrowful suffering upon us
and we will pay, and pay.

You said some ships escaped.

Where are they now?
Do you have clear intelligence?

Messenger

The surviving ships' captains spread their sails   480
and scattered to the winds, with no destination,
no order, mere panicked flight.

The army – what was left of us – started to die
in Boetician territory.
Gasping, breathless, ravaged by thirst – giving up
within crawling distance of a stream.

Some of us managed to get as far as Phocus,   485
Dorian country, and the Melian Gulf –
rich farmland, where the plains are irrigated
by the sweet plentiful waters of Spercheios.   490

And then on through Achaea and the towns of Thessaly

who took us in, starving as we were, who gave us food,
yet still more died, too weak to eat.

We staggered on: Magnesia, Macedonia,
across the river Axius and the reed marshes
of Lake Bolbe, to the mountains
of Pangaeus in the land of Edonia.
That night a god brought winter to autumn.

White-breathed, frost-tipped,
the stream of holy Srynon bound in ice.

Men who had never prayed before
now found their voice, falling on their knees to kiss
the earth, plea-bargaining, the night passing
in a thanks-giving that proved to be premature.

Prayers done, the army began to cross the river
where the ice was thickest.

Those of us who had set out before the sun warmed
reached safety, for soon it blazed.   505

Fissures in the middle channel cracked beneath feet

as the rays flamed, burning ice to water.

Soldiers raced, slipped, fell together, sank
beneath the jostling iceplates.
He who struggled least died soonest. A handful left.

We staggered on through Thrace,
little believing we would see our homes again.

We are all that's left, mere walking shadows,
returned to a land stripped empty of its men.

And all this is true and but a fraction
of the hatred God spat at the Persians.

~Messenger exits~

Chorus 2
We are trampled like grass,
God's heel grinds down on us.   *516*

Queen
Wretched.

Our army destroyed.

How prophetic my dream, how clear the warning,
how poorly you interpreted it!   *520*

You told me to pray, so I will pray
and pour oil, corn and honey from the royal store
to the gods above and the many dead below.
It's done.
The worst has already happened.
Nothing can reverse this fortune,

but I can trust in the future,   *525*

that some glimmer,
some hope will be there.

Your duty is to offer counsel,
so do your duty.

If my son returns, comfort him
and guide him to my door
lest he inflict on himself some further sorrow
to crown that which we already bear.

~Queen exits~

Chorus 1

Zeus, you took our army and its swollen pride

and smashed it to nothing.

The great city of Susa and Agbatana

you shroud in mourning.

Chorus 2

The women are crying,

shredding their clothes in grief.

Delicate hands beat breasts, bruising.

Tears soak the folds of their garments as together

freshly-made widows weep.   *540*

Chorus 1

The soft beds, the delight of youth, coupled joy:

Such pleasures will not come again.

Chorus 2

I feel the weight of the dead upon me.

Crushing.

Chorus 1

Crushing.

Chorus 3

It was that boy. That child we made King.

Xerxes took them.

Popo-ee   poppoi!*

Xerxes killed them.

Toto-ee   totoi!

Who else but Xerxes

mismanaged the whole campaign?

He trusted our all to ships,

and this the son of Darius

who did such little harm!

Our great leader, beloved, blameless.   *555*

Chorus 1

Foot soldiers, marines

sailed out on the twin-oared wings of death.

Ships took them

Popoi!

Ships slayed them

Totoi!

Ships destroyed them with their murderous thrusts
from Ionian hands.

Chorus 3

But the king escaped. The king slipped away
through the icy plains of Thrace.

Chorus 1

And those who were seized
by necessity died first.

        Pheu!   *Ehhh-e!*

Chorus 2

Pulped,

        O-aaah!

mangled,

fringing the shores of Cychreus' isle.   *570*

        Ah!

Chorus 1

Moan, bite your lips.

Chorus 2

Howl so it pains the heavens above to hear,

until our very flesh hurts.   *575*

Chorus 1

Razored by rocks

                    Pheu!

nibbled on, gnawed by the wordless swarms

                    Ehhh-e!

that children the pure sea.

                    O-aaah!

Chorus 2   *580*

And every house grieves,

lamenting the fate that the gods have sent.

Parents, suddenly childless, grow old

as they hear how their future died.

Chorus 1

The loss is too great.

Chorus 3

But who now in Asia will follow Persian rule?

Do you think they will still bend the knee
merely by the king's compulsion?
Or pay homage, bowing their face to the earth
to a power now utterly destroyed?   *590*

The monarchy is over.

Guarded tongues are freed.
The yoke has been lifted.
Liberation came
with the smashed skulls
on the battlefields of Salamis.

What remains of Persian might
is washed up in the tide
alongside our dead.

~Queen enters~

Queen
Friends,
those who know true suffering learn
disaster breeds panic, fear taints everything thereafter.
Yet in kinder times, we believe   *600*

the gentle breeze of fortune

will always blow our way.

We live now in a time of terror,

danger lurks everywhere.

The gods have turned their face away, and all I hear

is the din of catastrophe.

There's a fluttering in my heart.

I'm afraid.

And so come here alone, on foot, retracing the path

from my house but without majesty,

head bowed, a suppliant

meekly bringing offerings to the father of my child.

The dead need soothing.

I bring gifts to sweeten and mollify: 610

       pure milk, the radiance of honey,

       clear water from a virgin spring,

       fine wines from an ancient vineyard

       and from the eternally verdant olive tree

       its rich, scented oil,

       garlanded with wild flowers,

       the offspring of the earth.

Come, friends, let us speak the old words,

sing the songs of good omen.   620

Let us raise the dead.

Conjure up the soul of Darius
as I honour the earth and let it drink.

Chorus 1
Royal majesty, first amongst Persians,
send these gifts to the lower halls
while we entreat those   625
who guide and despatch the dead
to be gracious and smile on us.

Chorus 2
Earthly powers, dark spirits,
Hermes, King of Death,
release this soul into the light, above:
Darius, who of all mortals
may know a cure   630
and perhaps may speak.

Chorus 3
Can he hear?
Does the late king, equal of gods, know our pain?
Has this piercing sorrow penetrated even the grave?

Chorus 1

Lord of the dead, earth itself,

let him ascend from forgetfulness.

Let our Persian god, born in Susa,

rise from the dark slumber, below.

Release the divine Darius,

the likes of which no Persian soil has ever covered,   *645*

whose equal Persian soil never yet contained.

Chorus 2

He was loved, and so too is his grave

for the qualities of the nature it entombs.

Hades, send him up,

Aidoneus, release,   *650*

Bring our sacred Darius to us.

                    Ai   Ee-yeh!

Chorus 3

He never lost our men

to war-mongering acts of madness.

We called him God for he reigned

with god-like tolerance and wisdom.

Ai   Ehhh-e!

Sultan, Ballen, Shah of old, appear!

Rise with saffron-slippered feet   660

to the upmost pinnacle of your tomb.

Reveal your royal crest, sparkling diadem.

Come, harmless Darian, father of all.

Oi   O-ee!

Chorus 1

Hear now your childrens' pain.

Lord of all lords, appear.

The murk of hell covers us

for our young are dead.   670

Show yourself.

Come, harmless Darian, father of all.

Oi, o-ee!   Aiai, aiai!

Chorus 3

Much mourned since death took you.

Master, great Darius, why this double grief?

Who is to blame? Why did this happen?

Galleys, gone, three-banked ships, gone,

ships unshipped,   680

[68]

nothing left at all.

~Darius appears~

Darius

Faithful counsellors, you who were once young with me,

now elders of Persia: what troubles have beset our land?

The soil itself groans. I feel the scars.

There stands my widow at my tomb and I tremble,

dread bids me accept her offerings favourably.   685

And you, too, stand at my grave, with piteous

invocations shrill to wake the dead. I woke.

I came, as summoned, but the journey is not easy.

The gods below are skilled in taking, not releasing.   690

Authority alone bought me freedom, but the lease is short.

I am here. Waste no time. My stay is brief.

What burdens Persia with such dread and sudden weight?

Chorus 2

I can't look, I can't speak.

Chorus 1

How can I raise my gaze, or speak before you?

Reverence forbids it.

Chorus 2

I fear you now, as I feared, before.

Darius

You hooked me with your words and hauled me up.

Speak. Succinctly. Time passes.

Put by your old dread. Be brief.

Chorus 3

I'm frightened of displeasing you by speaking plainly,

and of such things...

Darius

That ancient fear has taken guard before your mind,

rendering you all speechless.

Lady, my once Queen, companion of my bed

when we were young: age clings to you.

Tears sully your face. Stop.

Speak to me.   705

What is life, but pain?

It stalks the land, salts the sea

and stings with every passing day of breath.

Queen

I envy you. You, of all mortals held the happiest fate.

When the sun shone on your face, you smiled,   *710*

and lived like a god, happy, prosperous, in peace.

I didn't envy you then, but I envy you now,

for dying before knowing defeat.

You shall hear the whole story, Darius,

succinctly, even briefly said:

Annihilation. Complete and utter ruin.

Darius

Was it pestilence? Civil war?

Queen

In Greece. Near Athens. Our entire host perished there.

Darius

Which of our sons led the army so far afield?

Queen

Xerxes. War lusting Xerxes, who emptied out a continent

'til there was nothing left.

Darius

The fool! Did he attempt this madness by land or sea?

Queen

Both. A double attack with twin armaments.

Darius

But how did an army of that magnitude cross?

Queen

By genius. He yoked the strait of Helle
and walked across.

Darius

He did that – calmed the great Bosporus?

Queen

He did. With divine help.

Darius

The same divinity that stole his mind.

Queen

Yes. As witnessed by the outcome.

Darius

What became of the men, to make you grieve so?

Queen

Destruction on land; destruction at sea.

Once the naval force was defeated,

the infantry were lost.

Darius

All died by the spear?

Queen   730

Why else would Susa mourn?

Darius

I grieve for them. Fine men,

our protectors, our strength –

Queen

And the Bactrian force, too. No survivors.

Darius

Wretched youth. To risk so much – so many –

the future of our allies, wasted.

How has this ended for him? Is he alive?

Queen

He reached with bitter relief the bridge

that yokes two continents together.

Darius

And has crossed in safety? Is it confirmed?

Queen

It's confirmed. The reports are accurate.

Darius

O-ee!

How swiftly the workings of the old prophecies

come true.

Zeus hurls their accomplishment at my son.

So soon. I hoped for longer, that the gods

would defer the oracle's fulfilment until a later time.

But when a man with zealous pride

hastens his own doom, the heavens

speed him along.

The fountain of misfortune overflows,

drenching, drowning all I hold dear.

And this, the achievement of my impetuous son,

youthful Xerxes, ignorant of his doings.

He hoped to stem the sacred Hellespont flow,   *745*

and bind in chains, shackled like a slave, God's property.

Turn sea to land against its nature,

fetter the waves with hammered chains,

then march his men across:

a mortal playing God to gods!   *750*

Was he possessed?

Surely this is the work of a fevered mind!

And now my life's work – prosperity, peace, power –

is plunder to the first comer's sword.

Queen

Don't blame him all. There were others –

the company he kept – bad company –

they taught him this way of thinking

and he listened well.

They made him feel a pallid moon, merely reflecting

the glory of your blazing sun.

Your father won riches, they said,

His prowess in battle! The valour! The might!

And what do you do but play warriors at home,

casting your spear aside,

spending what you never earned,

adding nothing to the power or inheritance.   755

What do you bring?

He was goaded to war,

slander driving him on

to mass his great armament

and march on Greece

to equal, if not exceed,

his father's achievements.

Darius

And what an achievement he made,

unsurpassed, unrivalled

in the history of Susa!

Never has such calamity befallen our people.

Not since Zeus first granted the honour

of one man reigning supreme

over the whole of Asia.

Medus was the first to lead,

succeeded by his son,

a reign of quiet and prudent reason.

Cyrus came third, the most blessed,

favourite of the gods,

who secured peace for his allies

as good sense helmed his fighting nature.

He obtained the peoples of Lydia and Phryga   *770*

and the whole of Ionia he subdued by force.

But the gods had no argument with him,

for he was wise.

His son, conqueror of Egypt, ruled fourth.

Fifth, Mardus, who disgraced both realm

and ancient throne.

We dispatched him quickly, a palace coup   *775*

led by the brave Artaphrenes.

Who now should be king? Lots cast. I won.

And I led forth many campaigns,

with multitudes of men,

yet I never achieved the great catastrophe of our son.

And now he rules.

He's young, unformed in mind

and forgetful of everything I instructed.

Counsellors, old comrades, be sure of this: *785*

Of all the kings who reigned, throughout the succession,

none has inflicted such manifest misery as this.

Chorus 1

What now, Lord Darius?

What can we do to restore good fortune?

Chorus 3

What course of action should Persia take?

Darius

None.

Do not campaign against the Greeks.   *790*

Lead forth no further expeditions on Hellian soil,

even if your numbers doubled theirs.

The land itself is their ally, and fights for them.

Chorus 2

Fights how?

Darius

Through famine.

By starving invaders whose numbers are too great.

Chorus 3

A hand-picked force then, small, well-equipped.

Darius

No. Not even the troops left stranded on Greek terrain
will gain safe passage home.

Chorus 3

What do you mean, sir?
The host has already crossed the strait into Europe –

Darius

– A few may return, a mere handful
if the oracle is to be believed,
and it has held true, so far,
and prophecies do not stop at half fulfilment.
If the old prophecy is true, Xerxes, chasing vain hopes,
will have left behind his personal regiment,
the choicest, hand-picked troops,
where Asopus and its tributaries water
the plain of rich Boeotian soil.
There they wait, and waiting with them is their ruin:
punishment for their proud and godless insolence.
Atonement for their arrogant swagger through Hellas, 810
smashing icons, burning temples, desecrating altars,
sacking shrines, leaving a trail of smoking rubble in what
had been the holiest of places.

Such sacrilege demands a price, and they will pay

in equal suffering.

Their well of grief will not run dry.

It gushes still, running red with Persian blood

scabbing the earth

congealing with slaughter

as lance after lance

pile after pile

heaps high the corpses

voicelessly screaming to us,   *820*

our children,

our childrens' children:

Witness. See, we died after all,

and mortals should cast aside such pride,

for arrogance blossoms to a fruit of ruin

and swells to its bitter harvest, tears.

Look on us and remember Athens.

Let no-one despising today's fortune

pour away their own prosperity

through greed for others' wealth.

For Zeus, the punisher of boastful thoughts stands by,

a stern and chastising auditor.

You're wise, my friends, so counsel Xerxes.

Explain this to him, correct his pride.   *830*

Heaven has warned him:

put off this rashness which offends

and provokes the gods.

As to you, my Queen, mother to our son,

fetch fine clothes befitting of his station

and go out to welcome him,

for grief has made him a beggar,   *835*

shredding his royal finery,

defaming the ceremonial dress,

reducing his status.

Speak kindly, gentle him,

for your voice alone, I know,

will be the only one he will hear.

But I must go, returning to the dark, below,

forgetfulness.

Old friends, farewell. Despite your grief   *840*

take pleasure in what remains – your life.

Wealth, pomp, and status mean nothing to the dead.

~Darius exits~

Chorus 1

How bitter to hear the countless suffering,

now and to come, which befalls the Persians.

Queen

This endless dirge that enters my soul.

But nothing gnaws so keenly as the thought of my son

clothed in shame, the rags of dishonour.

I will go in, and find clothing worthy

of his royal personage

and prepare a smile

and, smiling, go out to meet him   *850*

for I will not betray my own in these troubles.

~Queen exits~

Chorus 1

O popoi!

The life we once led in our well-run city,

wealth, ease, all that the earth yields

or laws upheld, was ours

when the griefless, gracious, never-harming Darius,

equal to God, ruled over us.

Chorus 3

The magnificence of our army, then!

Famed, honoured in the world's eyes.

We sacked the high citadels of our foes

and brought them down, lawful in battle,

the state guiding true

as our men marched back from foreign fields,

unscarred, unfatigued, to prospering, happy homes.

Chorus 2

The cities he stormed

without once crossing the Halys

or quitting native soil!

Chorus 1

Acheloian towns near the Strynon mouth,

Thracian settlements, and beyond the coast,

dry towns ringed with stone

all acknowledged him as king.

Chorus 2

As did the proud cities, perched high

above the Hellespont,

distant Propontis, the northern estuary,

blackest of seas.

Chorus 1

His were the surf-beaten islands

close to our shore.

Lesbos,

Chorus 2

the olive groves of Samos,

Chorus 3

Chios,

Chorus 1

Paros,

Chorus 3

Naxos,

Chorus 1   *885*

Myconos,

Chorus 2

Andros and neighbouring Tenos,

he ruled them all.

Chorus 1

And the seaward islands between Europe

and Asia: Limnos, where Icharus fell.

Chorus 2

Rhodes and Cnidus,

Chorus 1

the Cyprian towns Paphos and Soli,

Chorus 3

Salamis,

daughter to the city   *895*

which brings our downfall, now.

Chorus 1

And the teeming, prosperous cities

of the Greeks in Ionian territory

he reigned in majesty and understanding.   *900*

The untiring strength of warring men,

manifold allies of all races,

were his to command

and move as he wished.

Chorus 3

And now the reversal.

Crushed. Drowned. Conquered.

~Xerxes enters~

Xerxes

Io! Io!

Cursed, outcast, an evil thing,

bewildered at this savage fate

the gods hurl at me and the Persians.

My limbs are water,

all strength ebbs as I look at you,

old senators, wise.

Why was I spared the mercy of oblivion?

Your eyes and the faces of the slaughtered haunt me.

Despised, not even Death would take me.

I wish I'd perished with my men,   *915*

and that dirt now covered this hated face.

Chorus

Ototoi, o-toto-ee!

Chorus 2

Gone, Persia's honoured rule,

Chorus 1

the Empire,

Chorus 3

our glorious men, glittering in battle,

Chorus 1

our boast,

Chorus 2

our blossom,

scythed,

Chorus 1

mown down,

Chorus 3

mere grass.

Chorus 2

Asia cries for her youth

Chorus 3

slain by Xerxes

who crams Hell's jaws with our thousands dead

Chorus 1

thousands upon thousands

Chorus 3

ten thousand

Chorus 2

a million.

Chorus 3

Dead.

They marched away with Xerxes:

master archers,

skilled marksmen,

a forest of our youth

culled. Chopped down.

Chorus

Aiai, aiai!

Chorus 2

That protecting strength,

our shield, is gone.

We are bowed –   930

Chorus 3

the shame!

Chorus 2

– on our knees.

Xerxes

I did it. My fault.

Oioi o-ee!

Look at me: I am to blame.

The bane of the Persian people,

the curse,

blight of our nation.

It was me.

It was me.

Look: it was me.

Chorus 1

How can we greet you?

How can we receive you home

except in disaster's voice?

A howl of tears,

a Mariandynian dirge   939

whose very notes are pain.

Xerxes

Release it.

Send up voices raw with grief.

Shriek. Lament.

Roar until ear drums burst,

for God has a cruel and vindictive face

and is turned against me.

Chorus 1
Shrieking

Chorus 2
shrieking

Chorus 3
Wailing

Chorus 1
wailing

Chorus 2
The lament of defeat

Chorus 3
the clang and din for our drowned dead

Chorus 2

as a city mourns her lost sons.

Xerxes   *950*

It was the Ionians

and their armoured ships

that stole men's lives

and turned the tide,

slicing across the night-dark sea

to the unhappy, blood-dark shore.

Chorus   *955*

Oioitoi,   o-ee o-ee!

Chorus 1

Cry out. Learn all.

Chorus 2

But where are the others?

Your friends, our sons?

Chorus 3

Where are your close defenders,

the men who stand by you?

Pharandaces, Susas?*

Where is Pelagon?

Why is Datamas not with you?

960

Or Psammis and Susiscanes

who set out from Agbatana?

Why are these men not with you?

Xerxes

I left them

fallen from a Tyrian galley.

I left them

fallen and dying

off the shore of Salamis,   965

floating, swirling,

caught in the tide,

battered, pulped

against the rocks.

Chorus

O-ee o-ee, o-ee oioioi!

Chorus 1

And where did you leave Pharnuchus?

Chorus 2

Or brave Ariomardus?

Why is he not here?

Chorus 3

Where is Lord Seualces?

Chorus 1   *970*

Noble Lilaeus?

Chorus 2

Memphis?

Chorus 1

Tharybis?

Chorus 3

Masistras? Answer!

Chorus 2

Where are Artembares and Hystaechmas?

Chorus 3

Where? Account for them!

Xerxes

Io io ah me, yoh yoh mo-ee!

Hated Athens, hateful.

That gaping maw of death.

They saw the city, and in one stroke...   975

All are dead.

Chorus 3

And was it there the flower of Persia,

the King's Eye, faithful, trusted Alpistus,

Batanochus's son, was plucked out?

He who put numbers to men,   980

who counted out your thousands,

thousands upon thousands,

that true, accounting *Eye of Majesty* -

Did you leave him behind, too?

Chorus 1

And what of the son of Sesames?

Chorus 3

Or the son of Megabates?

Chorus 2

And Parthos and great Oibares...

Where did you leave them?

Chorus 1

Did you leave them?

Did you leave them behind too?

Chorus 3

Did you leave them behind to die,

killed by our enemies?

Chorus 2

Our poor men –

Chorus 1

Evil upon evil...

Chorus 3

Did you?

Chorus 1

... poured on the noble Persians.

Chorus 3

Did you leave them behind?

Xerxes

Yes! Yes!

They were my friends.

I long for them – fine, good men –

You name my friends and speak of evil   990

and stir and stir

and my heart tears and screams within my limbs.

Bo-a-ee, bo-a-ee!

Chorus 1

There are others, too.

More we need to know.

Chorus 3

Xanthes, marshall of ten thousand Mardians.

Where is he?

Chorus 2

And Anchares of the Aroi?

Chorus 1   *995*

Cavalry lords Diaixis and Arsaces?

Chorus 2

Egdadtes?

Chorus 1

Lythimnaes?

Chorus 3

And Tolmos of the tireless spear,

insatiable in combat.

Where is he?

Chorus 2

Where is your loyal retinue?

Chorus 1

Where are they?

Chorus 3

I am amazed, in all amazement

to find them not here,

not following in your royal train,

your tented carriage.

Did you leave them behind, too?

Xerxes

Yes.

Chorus 1

Warlords

Chorus 2

Generals

Xerxes

They have gone

Chorus 3

Commanders

Chorus 1

Marshalls

Xerxes

Nothing now but names

Chorus 2

Leaders

Chorus 1

Captains

Xerxes

All that led the Persian host are gone

Chorus 3

Thousands upon thousands

Gone.

Xerxes

I grieve and I mourn.

I mourn and I grieve.

Ieh, ieh! io, io!

Yay yay, yoh yoh![*]

Chorus

Yoh yoh, io io!

Chorus 2

Your powers strike us

with this unlooked-for doom.   *1005*

Chorus 1

Fate's ruin.

How cruel and clear your glare.

Xerxes

Struck. Whipped. Lashed.

Struck down from ancient good fortune.

Chorus 2

It hurts.

Xerxes

New pain.

Fresh torment.   *1010*

Chorus 1

Struck down by Ionian ships.

Chorus 3

Defeated.

Chorus 1

Our ill fate to encounter

their fierce, armed fighters.

Chorus 3

Truly defeated.

Xerxes

Our army, gone.

Persia's might, gone.   *1015*

Chorus 3

And you brought this upon us.

Chorus 1

Is there anything not wasted?

Is all lost?

Chorus 3

Did you lose everything?

Xerxes

You see these rags?

Chorus 2

Yes.

Xerxes

I have them.

And this quiver, for my arrows

– empty, now –

Chorus 1

And this you saved?

That's all? The sum of your kingly might

after such a vast store of weaponry?

Xerxes

There's no-one left to protect us.

Chorus 3   *1025*

The Ionian forces do not desert in battle.

They do not flee, nor flinch from spears.

Xerxes

They are too warlike,

too greedy for battle, they gorge,

hunger driving them on to kill.

Unforeseen –

I witnessed a massacre.

Chorus 2

When our ships were routed?

Xerxes   *1030*

I tore my clothes, shredding –

Chorus

Papa-ee, papa-ee! Papai, papai!

Xerxes

More! More than that!

Match my grief!

Chorus 2

Twice, threefold more!

Xerxes

We mourn.

They gloat.

Chorus 3

Strength shorn, razored away.

Xerxes

Naked.

Stripped of attendants.

Chorus 1

Drowned, now floating

in the sea which killed them.

Xerxes

Cry, wet your cheeks, howl

as we make our way home.

Chorus

Ai-ee, ai-ee!

My face is wet with tears

Xerxes

Cry out in response,

echo my pain   *1040*

Chorus

sorrow to sorrow to sorrow

Xerxes

Join in, bind your sounds with anguish to mine.
Sing pain.

All

Ototototototoi!

Xerxes

The misfortune is too great

Chorus

it crushes.
The pain.   *1045*

Xerxes

Beat, beat breasts. Arms row

Chorus 1

row on row on row

Chorus 2+3

sorrow to sorrow to sorrow

Xerxes

Echo cry to cry. Shrill.

All Chorus

sorrow to sorrow to sorrow

Xerxes

Your cries are my relief.

Chorus 1

We are nothing but tears.

Chorus 2+3

sorrow to sorrow to sorrow

Xerxes

Cry out, echo tears with tears.

Chorus 2

we weep

Xerxes

Shrill. Shriek.

Release voice.   *1050*

All

Ototottotoi! O-toto –toto-ee!

Chorus

bruise breast speak pain

Xerxes

Sing pain. beat bruise blow

Chorus

pain pain   *1055*

Chorus 2

On-nee-a; on-nee-a; on-nee-a; on-nee-a; on-nee-a*

Xerxes

rip hair tear beard

white hair wise gone

Chorus1+3

shred rip claw clench

Xerxes

shriek wail roar cry

Chorus 1+3

we follow we follow

Xerxes   *1060*

rip clothes gash breast

Chorus 1

sorrow to sorrow to sorrow to sorrow

Chorus 3

sing pain

Xerxes

pluck hair, rip – for them!

Chorus 3

thousands upon thousands

Chorus 1

youth gone we grieve we grieve

Xerxes

eyes wet heavy tears

Chorus 1+3   *1065*

crying crying

Xerxes

Echo my cry.

All chorus

Oioi oioi,   o-ee o-ee!

Xerxes

Home, home, wailing home.

All chorus

Yoh-yoh,   oi! Oi!

Xerxes   *1070*

Cry through the city.

All Chorus

crying crying

Xerxes

Every street, pain.

All Chorus

crying crying

Xerxes

Step lightly.

Chorus 1

pain in every step

Chorus 2

every step remembers

Chorus 3

step remembering pain

Xerxes   *1075*

Ehhh-ehhh-ehhh-ehhh!

The men the ships destroyed.

All chorus

Ehhh-ehhh-ehhh-ehhh!

our drowned our dead all gone

Xerxes

All gone.

All chorus

gone

Xerxes

Home, now; home, now.

All chorus

in tears, crying

in tears we lead you home.

end

First production of *Persians*
by National Theatre Wales, August 2010.

By: Aeschylus
In a new verse version by: Kaite O'Reilly

Director: Mike Pearson
Conceptual design: Mike Brookes
Design: Simon Banham
Music: John Hardy
Cast: Rosa Casado, Richard Lynch, Richard Huw Morgan,
John Rowley, Rhys Rusbatch, Sian Thomas, Gerald Tyler,
featuring Richard Harrington & Paul Rhys.

Characters

Chorus 1 – Head of state

Chorus 2 – Head of church

Chorus 3 – Head of military/defence

Queen

Messenger

Darius

Xerxes

Reviews

"Kaite O'Reilly's fine new version is spare, flinty and eloquent... This is great theatre... extraordinary, one of the most imaginative, powerful and haunting theatrical events of the year."

The Telegraph

"This is a theatrical experience like no other... chilling, terrifying and timelessly resonant evocation of the rending grief, fury, and devastation of war... O'Reilly's version is drenched in bloody poetry... Unique and unforgettable."

The Times

"... overwhelming... extraordinary... superb..."

The Guardian

Notes

Page 29 ~ Inspired by Cookson's translation, 1906.

Page 47 ~ Herodotus 8.75-8.76.1, as quoted in Loeb.

Page 50 ~ According to Herodotus (8.84) possibly to be
identified with Aeschylus's brother of the same name.

Page 61 ~ Variations of laments, spoken or sung by all chorus.
I've included them here as side text, marking
their placement in several translations.

Page 92 ~ Sousas.

Page 99 ~ Again, I am replicating various forms of cry from
different translations.

Page 107 ~ A rough phonetic pronunciation of 'pain'.